Contents

About the Author
Paul Fairclough is an FA-qualified coach who is currently manager of the England National Game XI. He is also a trained teacher.

DEFENDERS CAN WIN GAMES, TOO

Winning games of football is all about goals – scoring more than the opposition. But try looking at it another way… you will win if you concede fewer goals than the opposition.

Study any league table in the world, and you will see that the team with the smallest number in its 'goals against' column will be at the top of the table or thereabouts. So a successful football team has to have great defenders.

In Italy – a country that has taught the world the value of solid defending – there have been few better central defenders than Fabio Cannavaro or his international team-mate Alessandro Nesta. And Paolo Maldini has been an inspiration to a whole generation of Italian youngsters wanting to become full-backs.

Spanish kids have looked up to Fernando Hierro, the French to Lillian Thuram and Marcel Desailly. In the English Premiership, the likes of Sol Campbell and John Terry are idols.

But even forwards need to have the basic skills of defending. All good teams 'defend from the front'.

This means that, when they lose the ball, teams must get players between their own goal and the ball. So, your team's attackers are also your first line of defence.

It doesn't matter where you play on the pitch, you have to be a good defender, with a grasp of the necessary skills – tackling, marking, and passing.

We all marvel at the attacking flair of players like Welsh wing wizard Ryan Giggs, Italy's Francesco Totti and Frenchman Thierry Henry. We admire the all-round talents of David Beckham and the agility of a host of goalkeepers.

But defenders can be just as skilled – and just as important to the end result. The following chapters will show you how.

> It's not just attackers who can be clever — it's just that when defenders do their job well, you don't often see it. When they mess up, though, it's clear for all to see

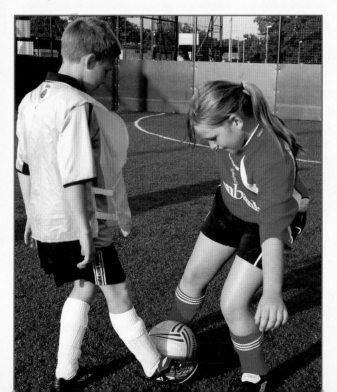

It's mine! Eyes on the ball, good balance and determination are needed to win the tackle

LONG, SHORT AND TALL...

Defenders come in all shapes and sizes. They are not all giants with thighs like tree-trunks and the flattest of foreheads. Height and bulk is a help if you are playing in central defence – and having to mark a bull of a centre-forward like Brazilian superstar Ronaldo or Christian Vieri, of Italy.

But some central strikers are speed-merchants. France's Thierry Henry and England's Michael Owen have pace to spare when it comes to taking on defenders. So speed on the turn, speed of thought – anticipation – and positioning, are just as important.

Full-backs must be able to head the ball against taller opponents. And they can win it, if their technique and timing is right.

Defenders need a whole range of qualities. The table below gives a list. Some are fairly obvious – and many apply if you are to be successful in any position on the pitch.

But there are specialist areas – like heading the ball for distance to clear your lines, and tackling without the ball falling free to another attacker – that we will look at in greater detail in the following chapters.

Keep calm: Good control and vision are key assets.

What qualities make a good defender?

- ■ **Calmness under pressure**
- ■ **Confidence**
- ■ **Courage**
- ■ **Quick reactions and feet**
- ■ **Mobility**
- ■ **Being decisive**
- ■ **Ability to 'read' the game**

Getting shirty: Brazil's Roberto Carlos, right, tackles a German forward.

As well as practice, you will improve if you watch and learn from better players. Look how much time better players seem to have on the ball. That is no accident. They do it by making sure they are always in the right position, and watching for dangers before they happen. Defending is sometimes uncomfortable – attackers will be foreceful in trying to get to the ball ahead of you.

This is where courage and strength come into it. But it is not all about muscle. While we think of attackers as being clever when they trick defenders to score, so defenders can be clever, too, with timing and positioning.

They don't always get the credit they deserve – just the complaints when the ball ends up in your net!

The basic need for teams is to score goals to win games. But, in order to score a goal, you have to have the ball. You can't score while the other side has it.

The more possession you have, the better your chances of scoring. You can win the ball from the opposition by picking up a pass that goes astray, or being first to a loose clearance, or you can tackle the player with the ball.

Tackling is an explosive action. But a smart defender will be patient and not dive in.

There is nothing more embarrassing than to be left on the floor, looking back as an attacker runs on to score!

You need to choose your moment – often when the attacker has knocked the ball a little too far to be in control of it. You will also need to keep him guessing about when you will challenge.

Here are some drills that will set you on the way to becoming a good defender.

Rope trick: Whip the top or piece of string away while your pal tries to step on it.

PRACTICE No. 1

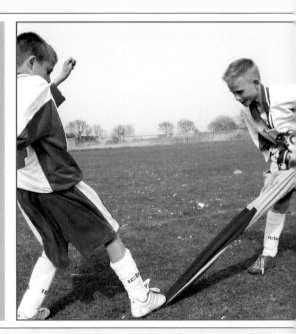

This is what I call the rope trick. You need two players and a metre-long piece of rope, or string. Even a training top will do.

- The attacker holds the rope facing the defender, and allows the end of the rope to touch the floor, just in front of the defender.
- The defender pounces forward to try to stamp on, or touch, the rope before the attacker can drag it away. This will test your reflexes!
- Allow the defender to have five attempts, then swap positions.

KEY POINT

The best position for the defender is to stand with the legs slightly bent at the knees, and shoulder-width apart. The body should be leaning forward slightly.

You should feel balanced and ready to move in any direction.

TIP
Any movement of any part of the defender's body will alert the attacker to whip the rope away.

7

TACKLING

NOW FOR REAL!

Let's make things more realistic. Mark out a pitch as shown in the diagram. Make each goal three paces wide. Use cones if you have them, though jumpers will do. Two of you are needed for this drill.

- An attacker starts with a ball on the edge of the pitch. The defender starts in the middle of the pitch. The attacker has five attempts to score in either goal.
- The defender must attempt to win the ball and force it off the pitch.
- After five attempts, change over.
- Keep your scores. Play three rounds in total to see who is the winner.

KEY POINT

The defender should be patient – don't dive in! Stay on your feet and see if you can work out which way the attacker is going to move. The best time to challenge is when he does not have the ball fully under control.

TIP
Pretend to move in one direction, to try to unsettle the attacker.

Generally, when you are in the penalty area and need to clear the ball with your head, you need to get as much distance on the header as you can.

All too often, weak clearances are picked up around the penalty area and smashed into the back of the net by hungry forwards!

It can be difficult, especially when you are being challenged as you try to clear, or a fellow defender gets in your way. It is about technique and timing.

A good defender can head the ball almost as far as some players can kick it!

He will try to put the ball into space, preferably where one of his own players can pick it up, or so that there is no immediate threat of another cross being sent back into his penalty area.

Watch the England defenders Sol Cambell and Rio Ferdinand. The leap for the ball, and the contact with the head, is all about timing. The best way to get maximum distance on a header is to use the energy of the ball to send it back in the direction it came from.

Heads up:
Keep your eyes open
when you head the ball
clear.

HEADING THE BALL

For this drill, we need two players and one ball. Mark out a small pitch, five paces long, with a goal three paces wide.

● An attacker stands with a ball in the middle of the pitch. He 'serves' the ball with his hands – just toss it up – so the defender can head it back over the attacker's head.

● The defender should try to score in the goal (this is a special goal – the cross bar is as high as the moon!) Height and distance are the aims.

● If the defender scores without the ball bouncing, he receives a bonus point.

● The attacker can try to prevent the goal by using his hands, like a goalkeeper.

● Have five goes each, then change over places. but don't acccept a poor serve that you can't head decently.

KEY POINT

● Head through the bottom half of the ball. This will send it high.

● Attack the ball – be aggressive. This will give the ball distance.

TIP

Keep your mouth closed to avoid biting your tongue!

*Practise:
Head it
back at the
server.*

FURTHER PRACTICE

Make a pitch 12 paces long.

● The defender can run from outside the area to head the ball.

● The same rules apply as before.

KEY POINT
Try leaping from just one foot.

Now extend the pitch to 15 paces.

● The attacker serves the ball either with a drop-kick from his hands (volley), or from the ground.

● The attacker serves from the goal. Remember, this goal has no crossbar, so you can head it as high as you like.

● Have five goes each and keep score.

KEY POINT
Arch your back and neck, and attack the ball.

TIP 1
Swing your arms in an upward motion to help you gain height. Be careful not to handle the ball.

TIP 2
As you are in the air, bend your knees and lift your ankles up towards your behind.

ACT LIKE A BLANKET

A defender often has to clear the ball first time in desperate situations. But there occasions when he or she becomes the first point of attack.

Then the defender must be able to bring the ball under control before delivering a precise pass. The best defenders have excellent ball control. No matter what height the ball comes to them, they can master it in a moment. Here is an mental image which will help you to understand what I'm getting at.

If you put a blanket over a washing line and then kicked the ball at the blanket, what would happen?

● The ball would hit the blanket and drop motionless to the ground

● The blanket absorbs all the energy of the ball by 'cushioning' it.

● The blanket caves in at the moment of impact and absorbs that impact.

If you want to 'kill' the ball then the part of the body that meets it must behave like the blanket and absorb all the energy of the ball, no matter the height.

PRACTICE No. 1

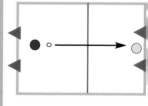

Set up a narrow pitch with goals three paces wide. You need two players and one ball. Both of you stand in a goal

- Using an underarm throw, try to score in the other goal. The ball cannot go above head height.
- Each player gains a point by preventing the goal, and controlling the ball before it moves one pace away.
- You cannot use your arms or hands!
- Have ten throws each.
- The winner is the player who secures the ball the most number of times.

KEY POINT

Be on your toes, ready to move in line with the flight of the ball.

Chest-trap: Don't push your chest at the ball, pull it away at impact so the ball drops at your feet.

TIP
Remember!
Cushion the ball like a blanket.

(5) PASSING

Pass it right: Use the instep to send an accurate long pass, though you can also use the out-side of your fot to apply 'bend' — spin.

HOW TO BECOME A PASS MASTER

If you thought passing was a skill best left to the creative geniuses, think again. It is a skill defenders need, too. You have already found out that the defender can be the first line of attack as he brings the ball out of defence, or if he wins a tackle and finds the ball at his feet.

But a good, accurate pass is essential if the attack is not to break down straight away. Not only that, a poor pass, straight to an opposing attacker, can leave your own defence wide open.

Passing is about keeping possession, and it is very much linked to the subject of the last chapter – control. Once you have comfortably secured the ball, you must then deliver an accurate pass to one of your team.

Defenders should generally pass to their team-mates' feet rather than into space ahead of them. Defenders have the advantage of being able to look ahead to see play develop in front of them, while attackers often receive the ball with their backs to goal.

However, the most important point to stress is that losing possession close to your own goal is a recipe for disaster.

That is why the defender must concentrate fully, in order to be accurate with his pass.

PRACTICE No. 1

10 paces | 10 paces

Player 1

Player 2

Take turns to pass through markers just one pace apart

Set up a pitch as shown. We need two players and one ball for this exercise.

● Each player stands 10 paces from a tiny goal, just one pace wide, in the middle of the pitch.

● Each player has 10 attempts to score by passing the ball through the tiny goal.

● Try five passes with the left foot, five with the right foot.

● The goal will be disallowed unless the ball goes through the goal and reaches the other player

● Have ten goes each. Keep your score: the winner is the player with most goals.

TIP
When you strike the ball, try to follow through with your foot in the direction of the goal.

KEY POINT
● **Keep your eyes on the ball.**

Try using your left foot and your right foot in turns to pass the ball. It will help make you a better player.

PRACTICE No. 2

Set up a pitch with two small side goals, each one pace wide, about 10 paces from the defender's goal and at an angle to it.

● The attacker tries to score in the big goal. He can throw or kick the ball, but it must be below head height.

● As soon as the attacker has made the attempt, he or she can run at the defender to prevent the defender scoring in either of the tiny goals.

● The defender is allowed a maximum of

three touches of the ball.

● Have five goes and then swap positions.

● Have another set of five goes. The most goals wins.

TIP

Try passing the ball into one of the tiny goals with your first touch.

⑥ PRESSING

CLOSING DOWN ATTACKERS' SPACE

When an opponent has the ball, your role as a defender means you must try to prevent him:

- Passing the ball forward to a fellow team player.
- Having a shot at goal.
- Moving forward with the ball.

The key in each case is to get close to the Aattacker as quickly as possible, and then assess the situation again. You must not give the attacker room to move, or time to think about his options. We call this 'closing down the space', or pressing.

The best defenders, like Spain's Fernando Hierro, and England full-back Ashley Cole, who is especially quick, close down the space in an instant. Poor defenders complain to their team-mates while an attacker nips between them and the ball rests in the back of their net!

Quick step: Get to the player with the ball as quickly as you can, to stop him making the most of the space and time he has to create danger for your team.

PRESSING

This drill will get you in the habit of 'closing the space down' quickly. Set up a pitch 10 paces square. Add a couple of goals as shown in the diagram.

● A defender, starting on the line with a ball, passes it firmly to the attacker.

● The attacker must have a minimum of two touches, and a maximum of three, to score in either of the two small goals.

● The defender should sprint forward to prevent the goal attempt.

● Have five attempts each, then try another five. Keep your score. The winner is the defender who prevents most goals.

KEY POINT
Sprint quickly once you have passed the ball.

TIP
When you get close to the attacker, slow right down.

Use a pitch 10 paces square with a goal at one end, four paces wide.

● The defender makes a firm pass to the attacker, and must then close the space down quickly .

● This time, make your run slightly curved. The attacker will probably move away from you instead of towards you – a natural response!

● You have started to dictate the attacker's moves and take control. Now try to guide him in one direction.

● Have five goes each, then another set of five. The winner is the one who prevents most goals.

KEY POINT
When you arrive at the attacker, don't dive in. Wait for him to lose full control of the ball, then make a tackle.

TIP
Throw the attacker a 'dummy' to make him think you are about to tackle.

When you get to the attacker, don't dive in to tackle – let him make a mistake.

Outnumbered: As soon as the striker gets the ball, he's faced by a defender and one of his pals.

SUPPORT YOUR TEAM-MATES

Football is a team game – but you don't just do things as one 11-player unit. There are at least three mini-teams working together in different areas of the pitch to make the whole team successful.

The back line will work together, talking to, and covering for, each other. So will the midfield and the forwards. If all the mini-teams are working well, then the team as a whole will do well.

There are situations on the pitch when you need to 'back-up' your mate, who might be struggling to cope with a tough opponent, or he may be outnumbered. That is when it is your duty to give him a hand. Assess the situation quickly to see where you need to be in order to help your pal out best.

If England's Wayne Rooney is about to take on a defender, you can bet that the defender's nearest team-mates will be there to offer their support.

DID YOU KNOW?

Former Arsenal defender Tony Adams made his England debut against Spain in 1987, alongside Glenn Hoddle. He later captained the England side managed by Hoddle.

PRACTICE No. 1

Mark a pitch 10 paces wide by 20 paces long, with goals four paces wide at either end. Two defenders take on one attacker.

● The defenders line up on the goal-line and one of them kicks the ball firmly to the attacker to start play.

● The attacker should attempt to dribble the ball through the defenders' goal.

● The defenders try to win the ball and dribble it through the attacker's goal.

● Have five goes, then each player changes position. The defenders who score most goals are the winners.

KEY POINTS
One defender should make a fast, curved approach to the ball.

Get sideways on to the attacker, 'inviting' him to move towards his 'trap'. The second defender should cover his mate. It means the first defender can afford to make a tackle, with his pal ready to steal the ball if it runs loose.

TIP
● Defenders should be on the 'balls of their feet'. A quick attacker can race past a defender who is back on his heels.

Waiting game: Don't dive in to challenge. Wait for the attacker to lose complete control of the ball.

COVERING YOUR MATES

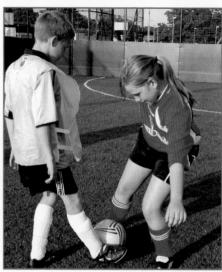

PRACTICE No. 2

This drill pits two attackers against two defenders on a pitch about 30 paces long.

● The defenders start together at one end and the attackers start together at the other.

● The game starts when the first defender passes the ball to either of the attackers.

● The game is over when the attackers have dribbled the ball over the goal line, or lost possession.

● Have five starts, then change roles.

KEY POINT

Be patient. If you miss a tackle, make a quick recovery behind your mate who is covering you!

Defenders must cover each other

Pass to start game

Attackers   **Defenders**

TIP

Watch the play as a whole and not just the ball.

USE YOUR BIG ADVANTAGE

When a forward receives the ball with his back to goal, it is important that he is not allowed to turn and attack.

As a defender, you have a big advantage. You are already standing between the attacker and your goal, and he is facing the wrong way. But it can all change in a moment. You have to be on your guard.

If players like Ronaldo, Ryan Giggs or Wayne Rooney are allowed to turn with the ball, they can cause chaos for the opposing team

It is vital that defenders concentrate at all times, and are ready to close down an attacker to stop him from turning.

DID YOU KNOW?

Fernando Hierro became Spain's all-time top goalscorer despite being a defender. He played in four World Cups and was an expert at long-range free-kicks. Hierro won European Cup glory with Real Madrid.

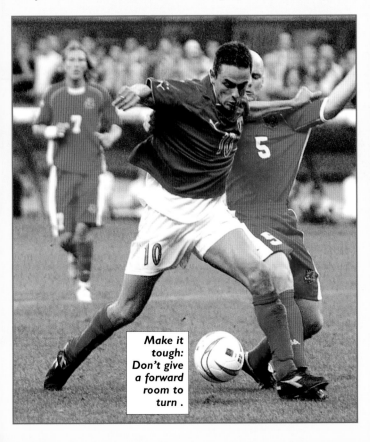

Make it tough: Don't give a forward room to turn .

APRACTICE No. 1

For this practice you need two players. You can use a wall – or another friend – to be the server.

● The attacker stands 10 paces from the wall. The defender starts with a ball 15 paces from the wall.

● The defender serves the ball by passing it firmly against the wall so that it rebounds to the attacker. The moment the ball hits the wall, both players are 'live'.

● The attacker has 10 seconds to try to dribble or pass the ball between the two markers.

● Have five goes each, and then repeat twice more. The winner is the defender who prevents most goals.

KEY POINTS

● Make up the ground quickly but stop about one pace from the attacker.

● Stoop down low so that you can see the ball from behind the attacker.

● Keep alert and on your toes, and make it difficult for the attacker to turn.

TIP
Don't get too close to the attacker, or he could roll his body against you and turn.

Be alert: Get to the attacker quickly enough to stop him turning.

Wall

Move to collect
ball when it
comes off wall,
then turn to
attack goal

attacker

defender

'Serve' to
start game,
then move to
stop attacker
turning

*Lean round
the attacker
to make
sure you get
a clear sight
of the ball.*

DON'T LET THEM TURN...

Set up a pitch 20 paces long with a goal at each end six paces wide. This is a two-a-side game. Each team has a defender and an attacker. You will need to mark a half-way line.

● Attackers play in their opponents' half, defenders in their own half. No player may cross the half-way line (see diagram).

● A defender must remain between the opposing attacker and the goal, unless his own attacker has the ball.

● When his attacker has possession he can 'support' him by getting ahead of the attacker he is marking to receive a pass, but he must stay in his own half.

● As soon as his attacker loses possession, he must ignore the ball and go back to his position behind the opposing attacker.

● The game is over when either team scores, or the ball leaves the pitch.

● Each team has five starts, then change roles with your team-mate, and start again.

KEY POINT
● Be patient: if you force the attacker to pass back to his defender you have done a good job.

TIP
● Stay alert, but don't expect to win the ball every time.

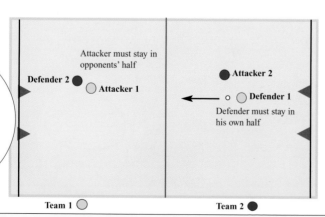

Attacker must stay in opponents' half

Defender 2 ● ○ Attacker 1

Attacker 2 ●

○ ○ Defender 1

Defender must stay in his own half

Team 1 ○   Team 2 ●

WHEN IN DOUBT, PUT IT OUT!

Playing football is about making decisions. Making the wrong decision on the pitch can have disastrous results!

If a defender makes the wrong decision, it quite often can result in a goal against his team.

Plenty of goals come from defensive errors. Watch a game in your local park, or on TV. Think about how a goal was scored. It isn't always down to the individual brilliance of an attacker…

When a defender is under pressure from an attacker he has to clear the ball. Often a defender will try to pass his way out of trouble when a good booted clearance upfield would be a better bet.

The best defenders do not take chances! There is an old saying in football: 'When in doubt – out!' In other words, if you are unsure what to do, always go for the safest option – the big, booted clearance. In this section, there are two drills designed to give you the feel and confidence of striking the ball.

Good volley: Perfect balance, eye on the ball.

CLEARANCES and VOLLEYS

You need a big area for this practice – well away from buildings with windows!

Stand no more than one pace from the goal-line of a goal with a net, or one pace from a washing line with a heavy blanket firmly secured to it.

● Hold the ball in your hands, let it drop to the ground and strike the ball forward. Have ten goes.

KEY POINTS
● Strike the ball with the laces part of your boot.
● Strike through the bottom half of the ball, not right under it.

TIP
● Keep your eyes on the ball as you make contact.

Power play: volley the ball as hard as you can.

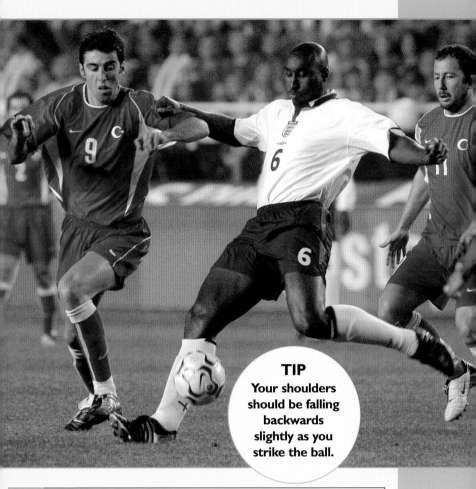

TIP
Your shoulders should be falling backwards slightly as you strike the ball.

PRACTICE No. 2

Stand one pace away from a goal or blanket, and turn sideways.

● A partner, no more than three paces away, serves you a ball from their hands. The serve should not be above knee height.

● Volley the ball into the goal or blanket using your right foot. Have five goes.

● Your partner then serves from the other side, so that you can practice with your left foot.

29

BE CONFIDENT ON THE BREAK

We have looked at clearing the ball while under pressure from an opponent. But if a defender is not under pressure he can bring the ball under control and start a counter-attack.

He can also use this tactic if he breaks up an attack with an interception or tackle. Rio Ferdinand of England and Sami Hyypia, Liverpool's Finnish defender, are very good at setting up counter-attacks. Watch games to see how confidently such players bring the ball out of defence. They don't look down at the ball – they look ahead for team-mates. Quite often, the other team will back off, giving the defender more time and space than they would give to an opposing forward.

A counter-attack should be swift and direct, leaving the opposition players stranded!

PRACTICE No. 1

Two defenders v two attackers. They line up in each half of a small pitch (see diagram). The defenders must stay in their half.

● The attackers try to run the ball across the defenders' goal line – they can't just kick it over it, but they can pass to each other.

● The defenders try to win the ball. If they do, they should attack quickly, trying to run the ball into the other goal (don't just boot it).

● If the attackers lose the ball, they must run back to defend their goal.

● When a goal is scored, or the ball goes off the pitch, the attackers start again with the ball.

● One game lasts three minutes. Then change teams.

KEY POINTS
● The defenders should try to anticipate the attackers' passes.

● A defender's pass to his pal should be quick and accurate.

Win ball then bring it out of
defence and pass to attacker

Defenders

Attackers
Attack one end first,
then the other.

Perfect poise: Look ahead at how the game is opening up – not down at the ball – when you start a counter-attack.

COUNTER-ATTACKING

This game is an extension of the last one. Two attackers agains two defenders.

● To score, the attackers must dribble the ball across the goal line – not shoot at the goal.

● If the defenders win the ball, they should try to score in the opposite goal by dribbling the ball across the line as before. But only one defender may cross the half-way line with the ball at any time.

● One defender should make a fast break into the other half, while the one with the ball looks to pass it to him.

● The game lasts for three minutes then reverse roles.

● Keep score – the team with the best goal-difference will be the winner.

Defenders

Half-way line

Attackers

KEY POINT

● When the defenders win the ball, they should react quickly.

TIP
The defenders should talk to each other at all times. Let your mate know where you are.

STAR TIP
● If it is unsafe to counter-attack, then 'clear your lines' – get the ball off the pitch!